This book belongs to

....

From a brilliant idea by Jenny Tyler

Edited by Gillian Doherty

First published in 2007 by Usborne Publishing Ltd,
83-85 Saffron Hill, London EC1N 8RT, England. www.usborne.com Copyright © 2007 Usborne Publishing Ltd.
The name Usborne and the devices ♀ ⊕ are Trade Marks of Usborne Publishing Ltd.
First published in America in 2008. UE. Printed in China.

How Big is a Million?

Anna Milbourne

Illustrated by
Serena Riglietti

Designed by
Nicola Butler & Laura Parker

Pipkin was a very small penguin
who was always asking very big questions.

How wide is the sea?

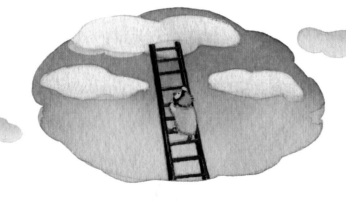

How high is the sky?

Is the moon made of cheese?

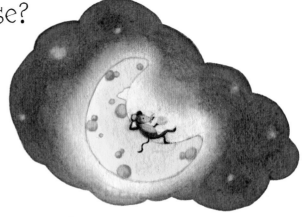

But the thing he wanted to know most of all was...

how big
is a million?

He went to ask his Mama,
but she was busy catching breakfast.

(It's important to have a full tummy
when you're asking such big questions.)

Pipkin counted the fish his Mama had caught
and found that there were...

TEN

"Ten's a big number of fish for breakfast," he said.
"But if ten's this big, how big is a million?"

"A million's more fish than you could ever eat," said Mama.
"A million's much, much more than ten."

Pipkin thought about this for a while.

He tried to imagine much, much more than ten.

"It's no good," he said at last.
"I'll have to go and find a million
to know for sure how big it is."

"Good luck," called Mama
as she watched him go.

Pipkin walked a little way and found a crowd of penguins.
They were huddled in a circle, keeping warm.

"That's a lot of penguins," Pipkin thought.
"There are much, much more than ten."

"Excuse me," he called. "How many of you are there?"

"A hundred," said the middle penguin.
"And I'm the warmest one of all."

"A hundred's a very big number," said Pipkin. "If a hundred's this big, how big is a million?"

"A million's much, much bigger than a hundred,"
the middle penguin said. "But a hundred is enough
to keep you toasty-warm. Would you like to join us?"

"No thank you," said Pipkin. "I have to find a million."

He set off again through the deep, white snow.

After a while his feet got tired of walking...

so he slid on his tummy down a long, steep hill.

He bumped into a seal cub
who was doing much the same thing.

Then ever so quietly it began to snow.

"That's a lot of snowflakes," Pipkin whispered. "There are more than a hundred and much, much more than ten. Do you think there are a million?"

"No," said the seal cub, "but I'm sure there are a thousand."

(And there really were!)

"A thousand is a really big number," said Pipkin.
"If a thousand's this big, how big is a million?"

The seal cub wrinkled his nose. "We-e-ell," he said,
"a million's much, much bigger than a thousand."

Pipkin and the seal cub
built a snow penguin...

and a snow seal cub...

and threw far too many
snowballs to count.

Then Pipkin said, "I really have to go. I have to find my million."

"Good luck," said the seal cub.

Pipkin walked and walked and walked...

...all around the South Pole...

...and back home again.

His toes were cold and he was sleepy all over,
and he hadn't found a million of anything at all.

Pipkin was a very, very disappointed penguin.

He said to his Mama:

"I found
TEN yummy fish,
a HUNDRED warm penguins,
a THOUSAND pretty snowflakes,
and a brand new friend.

But I couldn't find a million, however hard I tried."

Mama gave him a big, warm hug.

"Come outside," she said.
"I've got something to show you."

"Here's your million, my little Pip.
You can make a wish on every single one."

THIS WAY TO SEE
PIPKIN'S MILLION

OPEN THE
ENVELOPE TO SEE
WHAT PIPKIN SAW